Learning from Animals

The Many Ways to Be a FAMILY

Text by Tecnoscienza
Illustrations by Francesco Faccia

whitestar kids

CONTENTS

MANY FORMS OF LOVE

How can we ensure the safety of children so that they can grow up well and become strong? This is a question that all animals ask themselves, without being aware of it.

DIFFERENT SPECIES ANSWER THIS QUESTION IN DIFFERENT WAYS!

Some animals seem uncaring; they lay a significant quantity of eggs that they then abandon. However, making hundreds (or sometimes millions) of young is a good way to ensure that many of them survive dangers like predators.

MANY SPECIES, ON THE OTHER HAND, HAVE LOVING MOTHERS AND FATHERS...

...even if not in ways we would expect. Some parents only build safe dens and guarantee food for their young, without even giving them a glance. But there are many that focus entirely on care, giving their babies love and unconditional affection.

LET'S FIND OUT MORE...

OCTOPUSES

SCIENTIFIC NAME:
Octopus vulgaris

The mother octopus dedicates everything to raising her young.

SINGLE PARENT

The mother octopus sacrifices everything for her offspring. When she feels ready to lay her eggs, she scans the seabed for a sheltered spot: a crevice or a crack between rocks, but also among car tires or aluminum cans. Anything goes. The important thing is that the spot is safe. She then begins to lay hundreds of thousands of small eggs that look like soft whitish balloons with a string, a bit like the balloons you see at parties. With no help—the male does not participate in any way—mother octopus carefully intertwines thousands of eggs, creating bunches that she cautiously attaches to the walls of the chosen spot. Then she begins to clean them, touching them delicately with her tentacles and blowing fresh, oxygenated water over them.

SHE DOES THIS FOR MONTHS AND MONTHS, WITHOUT REST, WITHOUT THINKING ABOUT ANYTHING ELSE, WITHOUT EATING.

MOTHER'S HEARTS
The octopus has three hearts, a main one and two others near the gills.

WHEN THE BABIES HATCH AND BEGIN TO SLIP AWAY, FOLLOWING THE CURRENTS OF THE VAST SEA, THE SATISFIED MOTHER OCTOPUS CAN FINALLY CLOSE HER EYES, FOREVER.

THEY WEIGH
up to 19.8 lbs (9 kg).

THEY LIVE
in the Mediterranean Sea, and in all the world's oceans.

A SHORT AND INTENSE LIFE
They live up to two years and are considered the most intelligent sea animals.

DISCUS

SCIENTIFIC NAME:
Symphysodon spp.

Discus parents take turns feeding their offspring with their own bodies.

EQUAL PARENTS

It often happens among fish that babies, from birth, have to look for food on their own. This is because the parents are too big and the mouths of the young are too small; how could dad and mom feed their baby fish, considering that they only have fins? This is not the case among the discus fish that live in the Amazon River. The fathers and mothers of this beautiful, brightly colored species go for a swim surrounded by a cloud of dozens of young who wave their little fins like many shiny flags. The little ones are all having breakfast on the round bodies of their parents, as a delicious and abundant flow of mucus comes off of the adult fish. It is a meal for the little ones, rich in highly nutritious substances that are essential for their growth.

A LONG BREAKFAST
The babies are fed for two to four weeks of their life, then they are independent.

THE PARENTS TAKE TURNS IN THEIR TASKS: WHEN MOM GOES HUNTING, DAD FEEDS THE CHILDREN.

THEY WEIGH
about 7oz (200 g).

LENGTH
up to 6 inch (15 cm).

THEN, WHEN MOM COMES BACK FROM WORK, IT'S AN IMMEDIATE CHANGING OF THE GUARD AS SHE TRANSFORMS HERSELF INTO A TABLE SET WITH FOOD.

THEY LIVE
in the waters of Brazilian lakes and rivers.

GORILLAS

SCIENTIFIC NAME:
Gorilla gorilla

One male, many females, and a group of offspring is the most common family among mammals.

MANY MOTHERS AND MANY HALF-SIBLINGS

A typical gorilla family consists of a father, many mothers, and a good number of young who scamper around. Growing up as a young gorilla means wandering around the forest constantly playing with their half-siblings under the watchful eye of their mother and their father's other partners. The females are the ones who look after the babies. The male, on the other hand, does something else. He is a large ape with a muscular gray back—a color that attests to his venerable age—who sometimes grants a gesture of affection toward his offspring, for example, by removing insects from their fur. But he is generally busy leading the group in the African forest, beating his chest, roaring, and showing his long canine teeth to intruders.

A LIFE ON THE MOVE
Families cover a distance of up to 0.6 mile (1 km) a day in search of food.

THE BABIES GROW UP IN THESE NOMADIC FAMILIES, WHICH MOVE AROUND IN SEARCH OF FOOD.

THEY LIVE
in the forests between Cameroon and Congo.

WHEN THEY ARE ABOUT EIGHT YEARS OLD, THE BABIES ARE READY TO GO OFF ON THEIR OWN.

HOW MANY ARE THERE?
Each group can consist of up to 12 gorillas.

I WANT TO SLEEP ALONE!
A small gorilla sleeps alone from three years of age.

BEAVERS

SCIENTIFIC NAME:
Castor spp.

Beavers are loving parents and are attentive to their offspring.

A VERY CLOSE-KNIT FAMILY

The fathers of herbivorous mammals very often are not involved in the care of their young. Since eating vegetables provides very little energy, males with this diet prefer to spend the whole day grazing on grass; this way they can stay strong and protect their territory. Among herbivores, male beavers are an exception, as they are very involved fathers. These animals do not eat simple grass or shrubs, but rather trees, very high-energy food that beavers manage to store in the ponds behind their dams. Therefore, having a pantry full of excellent food to munch on provides the beaver family with a lot of time and allows them to be very close-knit. Both parents take care of the babies, in addition to the older siblings who often bring tasty pieces of bark to the younger ones who cannot yet leave the den.

TWO TYPES OF BEAVERS
There is a North American species and a Eurasian species, which lives mainly in Scandinavia and Russia.

THE FAMILY
can reach up to 10 individuals.

AS SOON AS THE BABIES ARE OLDER, THEY BEGIN TO TAKE A LOOK OUTSIDE.

AND WHEN THEY CAN, THEY JUMP ON THE BACK OR ON THE BROAD TAIL OF THE FATHER BEAVER TO GO AND EXPLORE THE LAKES AND MANY CANALS THAT SURROUND THEIR HOME.

NOT ONLY LOGS
Beavers also eat leaves and roots of aquatic plants.

ETERNAL LOVE
Beavers are monogamous for life.

JACANAS

SCIENTIFIC NAME:
Jacana spp.

Jacanas form a rare type of family, but a very effective one in protecting their young.

A MOTHER AND MANY FATHERS

The female jacana—a long-legged bird that lives in ponds and swamps in the Americas—chooses the best males. Yes, *males*, plural. In nature, although rarely, there are some families with one mother and many fathers. The mother jacana generally chooses up to four partners, all smaller than she is; their task is to build floating nests on the water, which sometimes stand directly on delicate water lily leaves. The female jacana looks at the nests made by the males, selects the ones she thinks are best, and lays her eggs there. Then she leaves the eggs to be incubated by her partners. When the eggs hatch, it is always the fathers who look after the chicks. They dedicate themselves to finding food and caring for and educating the chicks. The mother jacana patrols the territory.

A STRANGE BIRD
Birds normally raise chicks in pairs.

THE FAMILY
can have up to 16 chicks per clutch.

WHEN A SNAKE OR OTHER PREDATOR APPROACHES THE CHICKS, THE MALES SHRIEK IN ALARM.

THEY LIVE
in Central and South America.

THE MOTHER RUSHES AGGRESSIVELY TO SAVE EVERYONE, DRIVING THE ENEMY AWAY WITH AGGRESSIVE PECKS.

WALKING ON WATER
They have special legs capable of walking on water lilies.

EMPEROR PENGUINS

SCIENTIFIC NAME: *Aptenodytes forsteri*

The male emperor penguin keeps his only egg warm for two months.

DADDY'S WARMTH

When the mother penguin heads to the cold waters and goes hunting for fish, the father penguin stays on the ice with the egg. In an environment that can reach minus 65 degrees Celsius, his job is to keep the egg warm by preventing it from even briefly touching the ground. If that were to happen, it would be the end; the egg would freeze and the chick would die.

The father penguin therefore insulates it by keeping it balanced on the tops of his feet and at the same time manages to warm it with his body. And to get even more warmth, he huddles together with thousands of other fathers who do the same. This enormous group remains in the same position for 60 days and 60 nights, without protection and without food, dedicating themselves entirely to their eggs.

FEEDING
The father penguin is able to produce a kind of milk for the chick.

WHEN THE MOTHER RETURNS, THE CHICK HAS OFTEN ALREADY BEEN BORN.

HOW THEY DO THE HUNTING
Father and mother look for fish up to 330 miles (500 km) away from the nest.

WHEN THE MOTHER RETURNS, THE FATHER CAN FINALLY GO AND EAT SOMETHING, AND THEN THE COUPLE BEGINS TO RAISE THE CHICK TOGETHER.

THEY LIVE
in Antarctica.

THEY GROW BIG
The chicks are independent after four months.

THE WEIGHT OF THE FATHER IS
44-88 lbs (20-40 kg). While incubating he loses 33 lbs (15 kg).

BLACK ANTS

SCIENTIFIC NAME:
Lasius niger

Like all ants, the black ant lives in dense and populous all-female families.

A MOTHER WITH THOUSANDS OF DAUGHTERS

In that teeming family inside an anthill, no ant has ever met its father. Actually, no ant has ever even known it had a father. And it's completely natural because when their mother met their father, it was a quick date, lasting the blink of an eye. After fleeting encounters like this one, the queen ant begins her family. On the ground, after she has abandoned her wings, she starts to dig the first tunnel of her den. Then, in the darkness of the subsoil, she begins to lay eggs that were fertilized with the semen, which she keeps inside her body, of the males she mated with. From then on, she lays eggs in an orderly fashion, without ever going out into the open air again.

THE LARGEST COLONY ON EARTH
is that of the Argentine ant (*Linepithema humile*), spanning from Italy to Portugal.

FROM THE EGGS, IN ADDITION TO A FEW MALES DESTINED TO HAVE VERY SHORT LIVES, THOUSANDS AND THOUSANDS OF FEMALES ARE BORN EVERY YEAR

JUST LIKE ANTS
Some bees and wasps, from which ants descend, have similar family structures.

THESE FEMALES ARE THE ONES WHO TAKE CARE OF EVERYTHING, AS WELL AS CARE FOR THEIR OLD AND GIGANTIC MOTHER, WHO IS BUSY LAYING EGGS UNTIL THE LAST MOMENTS OF HER LIFE.

LARGE FAMILIES
Colonies can reach up to 40,000 individuals.

BABY ANTS
are born as larvae then become white.

HOW LONG DOES A BLACK QUEEN ANT LIVE?
Up to 20 years.

BROWN-HEADED COWBIRDS

SCIENTIFIC NAME:
Molothrus ater

These birds abandon their eggs, but that doesn't mean they don't care about the little ones.

FATHER AND MOTHER AWAY, APPARENTLY

The female cowbird, after being fertilized by a male, looks to get rid of the newborn. It never occurs to her to make a nest. In fact, her plan is to find the nest of another species of bird—she prefers bowl-shaped ones—in which to lay her egg and then fly away, hoping that her baby will be raised by others. When this plan succeeds, a bizarre scene occurs in which different chicks live together in a nest without the new parents realizing that they are feeding an intruder. However, the mother cowbird's plan does not always succeed; sometimes the other birds notice the extra egg and destroy it. This can unleash terrible revenge if the mother cowbird notices. She will rush to the nest, destroying it and breaking any other eggs that are in it.

WHY ARE THEY CALLED COWBIRDS?
Because as adults, these birds often follow grazing animals.

THEY LIVE
in North America.

THIS SHOWS THAT EVEN THIS APPARENTLY DETACHED MOTHER STILL WORRIES ABOUT THE FATE OF HER OFFSPRING.

AWAY FROM THE NEST!
After about two weeks the chicks are ready to join a flock of cowbirds.

DIMENSIONS
length: 6-8 inches
(15-20 cm)
weight: 1-2 oz
(30-60 g).

HORNBILLS

SCIENTIFIC NAME:
Bucerotidae spp.

The way in which hornbills protect their offspring is truly extreme!

AS LONG AS THE CHICKS ARE SAFE!

In their early years, young hornbills live in a kind of prison lit only by a small sliver of light. It is the typical nest made by hornbills, a large family of birds that live in the tropics. The nest is built by the mother hornbill who, well before laying her eggs, locks herself in a cavity in a tree that she then seals, often with the help of her partner, by creating a wall made of mud, excrement, and chewed fruit. Only a narrow opening is left in the wall. The mother hornbill remains locked up and can lay her eggs without disturbance, and within a month, the chicks will hatch. The father hornbill, on the other hand, goes hunting. His job is to stick his large beak into the slit to provide his family with fruit, insects, or small reptiles to eat.

HOW MANY SPECIES ARE THERE?
There are more than 50 species.

FOR MORE THAN A HUNDRED DAYS THE FATHER WILL NOT SEE HIS OFFSPRING: HE WILL ONLY HEAR THEIR FAINT CHIRPING.

EGGS
They can lay up to eight eggs.

THEY LIVE
in Africa and tropical and subtropical Asia.

WHEN THE CHICKS GROW FEATHERS, THE MOTHER HORNBILL BREAKS DOWN THE WALL AND THE FAMILY IS FINALLY ABLE TO REUNITE.

THE LARGE BEAK is equipped with a "helmet" that makes it harder.

THREE-SPINED STICKLEBACKS

SCIENTIFIC NAME:
Gasterosteus aculeatus

The male stickleback takes care of his offspring without a partner but with great energy.

A SINGLE FATHER WHO DOES EVERYTHING

Dad stickleback wants to do as much as he can by himself. He builds the nest—a sort of small, elongated underwater igloo—nervously gathering roots and aquatic plants that he finds on the bottom of the river and cements them with a substance that comes out of his kidneys. Then he lures one or more females into this nest to make them lay eggs. As soon as they have done their duty, he immediately chases them away.

Then he opens windows in the nest to better oxygenate the eggs and ventilates them by continually shaking his pectoral fins. Finally, he stands guard, sharpening his gaze and scanning every corner of the river, and chases away any intruders until the eggs hatch.

WHEN DO THE YOUNG BECOME INDEPENDENT?
Generally two weeks after hatching.

ONCE THE BABIES ARE BORN, DAD STICKLEBACK BECOMES EVEN MORE AGGRESSIVE. HE REPELS AND FURIOUSLY CHASES ANY PREDATOR THAT DARES TO APPROACH HIS HOME.

DIMENSIONS
normally 1.2-2 inches (3-5 cm).

IF CORNERED, HE LETS THE BABIES SWIM INTO HIS MOUTH TO PROTECT THEM. ONLY WHEN THE DANGER HAS PASSED, DOES HE SPIT THEM OUT.

THEY LIVE
in fresh water and on the marine coasts of the Northern Hemisphere.

NUMBER OF EGGS
From a minimum of 50 to a few hundred.

MOUNTAIN ENTRANCE
The sentries are positioned on an earth mound.
EMERGENCY ROOM
They don't stay there for long, just until everything is safe again.
PUP ROOMS
SOCIALIZATION ROOM

EVERYTHING BELONGS TO EVERYONE!

MOST PRAIRIE DOG FAMILIES CONSIST OF A FATHER AND TWO OR THREE MOTHERS WITH THEIR PUPS, BUT THERE MAY BE LARGER FAMILIES WITH TWO FATHERS AND MANY MOTHERS AND PUPS OF VARIOUS AGES. EVERYTHING IS SHARED: EVERY ROOM AND EVERY SUPPLY IS COMMUNALLY OWNED.

PRAIRIE DOGS

SCIENTIFIC NAME:
Cynomys ludovicianus

Large and very organized families!

LARGE FAMILIES

Although the open American plains may look like endless expanses of grass where not many animals live, underground live numerous families of rodents that dig continuously and move quickly in the darkness of their tunnels. Whenever they can, they rub their faces together as a sign of affection. These animals are called prairie dogs, and the adults are about the size of rabbits. They live in large families organized just like cities. Each family community has an "apartment," and the various apartments are close to each other. The prairie dogs access them through underground holes.

THEY ARE NOT DOGS!
They got the name because they "bark" like small dogs.

THEY LIVE
in the prairies of North America.

THE LARGEST PRAIRIE DOG CITY KNOWN was in Texas. Approximately 400 million individuals lived there.

HOW MANY FAMILIES? Usually a city hosts about 20 to 25 families.

LISTENING ROOM
To hear noises and vibrations from outside.
THE FATHER IS ALWAYS ON THE ALERT. IT MAY HAPPEN THAT SOME OTHER FAMILY TRIES TO STEAL THEIR APARTMENT. AND IT IS NOT UNCOMMON FOR ATTACKS TO COME FROM CLOSE RELATIVES!
WAREHOUSE
Crammed with nutritious grass.

BEDROOM
They go there to rest.

SOCIALIZATION ROOM
Here they play and cuddle by rubbing their noses together in a kind of affectionate kiss.

PUP ROOMS
These are the most protected rooms. Each mother takes care of her pups, but it is not uncommon for them to be nursed by other females.

AMERICAN BURYING BEETLES

SCIENTIFIC NAME:
Nicrophous americanus

The environment where the larvae of this insect grow is cared for extremely well.

AN UNEXPECTEDLY WELCOMING HOME

The mother and father American burying beetles meet on top of the corpse of an animal, usually a recently dead mouse or bird. They carefully remove any hair or feathers, then make a ball of its remains and bury it at the bottom of a dark tunnel. This will be the love nest in which they will form their little family. Mom lays her eggs in a hollow on top of the corpse. While waiting for their young to be born, both parents keep the carcass free of fungi by scraping it off with their mandibles and sterilizing it with a disinfectant that they produce from their abdomens. When the larvae are born, they find excellent food ready to eat, even if they won't be able to eat it right away.

ANTENNAE
They function as receptors for rotting flesh, which the beetles can sense from 1.8 miles (3 km) away.

UNTIL THEN, THEIR PARENTS WILL TAKE CARE OF THEIR FEEDING DIRECTLY, SQUIRTING A DARK LIQUID FROM THEIR MOUTHS.

THEY ARE
1.2-1.4 inches (30-35 mm) long.

AFTER A WEEK SPENT EATING UNDER THE WATCHFUL ANTENNAE OF MOM AND DAD, THE LITTLE ONES ARE READY TO BEGIN THEIR METAMORPHOSIS AND BECOME ADULTS.

THEY LIVE
in North America, far from human communities.

FAMILY SIZE
Up to 30 larvae per pair.

AFRICAN WILD DOGS

SCIENTIFIC NAME:
Lycaon pictus

African wild dog families adopt parentless puppies.

FOR PUPPIES LOOKING FOR A NEW FAMILY

Wild dog pups know they can count on every member of their pack, a large family made up of mom and dad, but also dozens of other adults: aunts, uncles, and older brothers and sisters who act as helpers and take care of them whenever they can. They do so even in the unfortunate event that the pups' parents die; wild dogs, in fact, have an extraordinary propensity to not abandon the weakest to their fate. This also happens if a pack of wild dogs encounter pups that have lost every adult they can rely on, perhaps killed by a lion, and who wander alone in the savannah. The larger animals, even if they are not relatives, immediately welcome and feed the orphans just as if they were part of their own pack.

A PACK OF WILD DOGS can consist of 20–30 adults, but the pups come from a single pair.

IT IS A REAL ADOPTION.

THEY LIVE in sub-Saharan Africa.

THE LITTLE WILD DOGS GROW UP IN THEIR NEW FAMILY, WHERE THEY WILL LEARN TO HUNT WILDEBEEST AND ANTELOPE AND CONTRIBUTE TO THE WELL-BEING OF THE ENTIRE GROUP.

LIVING IN A FAMILY is essential. Wild dogs die if they are separated from the pack.

THE YOUNG ARE IMPORTANT! The youngest of the pack always eat first.

FLORIDA SCRUB JAYS

SCIENTIFIC NAME:
Aphelocoma coerulescens

Blue jays often help relatives who have offspring.

THEY HELP EACH OTHER IN THE FAMILY

In Florida scrub jay families, there is more than just a father, a mother, and a clutch of chicks. That would be too simple. In one out of two families of these blue-feathered birds, in addition to the two parents, there are also young jays who help by constantly bringing lizards or crunchy insects to feed the chicks. And there are others ready to bring twigs to fix the nest and others that act as sentries, their eyes permanently fixed on the horizon, ready to sound the alarm if they see a buzzard or sparrowhawk.

THE HELPERS
Generally after two or three years they start their own family.

ALL THESE INDIVIDUALS, MALE AND FEMALE, ARE THE *HELPERS*: YOUNGSTERS CLOSELY RELATED TO ONE OR BOTH OF THE PARENTS.

THEY MEASURE
about 8-10 inches (20-25 cm).
THEY WEIGH
on average of 3 oz (80 g).

THE CLANS
include up
to eight jays.

OFTEN THEY ARE OLDER BROTHERS AND SISTERS OF THE CHICKS, TOTALLY DEVOTED TO THEIR PROTECTION.

THEY LIVE
in the scrublands
of Florida in
North America.

CROCODILES

SCIENTIFIC NAME:
Crocodylus niloticus

A rare case among reptiles, these animals protect and care for their young.

THE WARM KISS OF A COLD-BLOODED MOTHER

The jaws of the Nile crocodile are among the strongest in the world. This animal's bite is four times stronger than that of the great white shark, and it's capable of tearing off the leg of a large animal like a lion. Yet, when it comes to her offspring, the jaws of a mother crocodile are extremely delicate. Her enormous, cavernous mouth turns into a safe den for the little crocodiles. She goes for a walk with her babies in her mouth, who stick their heads out between her teeth. Mother crocodile takes extraordinary care of her young, starting from when she lays her eggs.

VIGOROUS YOUNG
They are ready to leave the nest when they turn two, and they exceed 3 feet (1 m) in length.

THESE ANIMALS, ALONG WITH CAIMANS AND ALLIGATORS, ARE AMONG THE FEW REPTILES THAT BUILD A NEST AND DEFEND IT FROM PREDATORS, A BEHAVIOR THEY SHARE WITH BIRDS AND MAMMALS.

SCALY NEWBORNS
They measure 0.11 inch (300 mm) at birth.

THEY LIVE
in central-southern Africa.

IF NESTS ARE CLOSE TOGETHER, THE MOTHER CROCODILES MAY ORGANIZE THEMSELVES TOGETHER TO GUARD ALL THE YOUNG, LIKE A LARGE NURSERY.

AND DADDY CROCODILE?
He takes care of protecting the territory.

DUNNOCKS

SCIENTIFIC NAME:
Prunella modularis

This hedge sparrow loves to experiment with many types of families.

MANY FAMILIES. ALL DIFFERENT!

If you wander from branch to branch in any grove populated by this sparrow, you can find many families that are all neighbors but all different. There are nests with a male and a female who, like most birds, lead a quiet life incubating eggs, while next door a sparrow feeds her chicks along with two partners. Then a few feet away, a male sunbathes together with his two female partners.

Just a little farther on, there is a family in which the chicks are raised simultaneously by three mothers and two fathers. And elsewhere there are nests in which the chicks are cared for by six different parents.

HOW MANY EGGS?
In each nest there are three to five eggs.

THEY LIVE
in Europe and Asian Russia.

ALL THESE FAMILIES HAVE ONLY ONE GOAL: TO INCUBATE THEIR BLUE EGGS AND RAISE HEALTHY CHICKS ONCE THEY HAVE HATCHED.

MEASURES
up to
6 inches
(15 cm).

IT NESTS
in bushes
and conifers.

THE FAMILIES IN WHICH THERE ARE SEVERAL FATHERS AND SEVERAL MOTHERS SEEM TO BE THE MOST EFFECTIVE ONES BECAUSE UNITY IS STRENGTH!

LAYSAN ALBATROSSES

SCIENTIFIC NAME:
Phoebastria immutabilis

Two females are best to raise all the chicks.

A FAMILY WITH TWO MOTHERS

On the coasts of the Hawaiian Islands, where the blue of the sky merges with that of the ocean, live the families of Laysan albatrosses. Many of these familes, up to three out of ten, are made up of two mothers who, during the mating season, build cozy nests on the golden sand, collecting twigs and seaweed to house their future chicks. Even if they don't have a male to mate with, they don't lose heart. With a bit of luck, they manage to find one far away who can fertilize their eggs. Then, after over two months of incubation, when the chick hatches, the two mothers take turns warming it and feeding it with small crustaceans from the sea. These special families seem to form when males on the islands are scarce.

IN THIS WAY, BY CREATING FAMILIES WITH FEMALE PARENTS, THE ALBATROSSES MANAGE TO INCUBATE AS MANY EGGS AS POSSIBLE.

DIMENSIONS
32 inches (80 cm) long, with a wingspan of almost 6.5 feet (2 m).

A LONG LIFE
Some individuals live over 70 years.

AND SO EACH CHICK IS GUARANTEED ALL THE LOVE AND CARE IT DESERVES.

NOT ONLY HAWAII
Some individuals of this species also live on Mexican and the Japanese islands.

FLAMINGOS

SCIENTIFIC NAME:
Phoenicopterus spp.

Hundreds of adult flamingos look after the chicks as they play.

AN EXTENDED FAMILY

When its egg breaks open, the flamingo chick comes out and looks at the world for the first time. The first thing it sees are the large, curved beaks and loving eyes of its parents. In the flamingo family, both father and mother take care of the little one, who at this age looks like a white and wobbly tennis ball, with two beautiful pink legs sticking out from underneath and, on top, a pointed beak. The parents feed it with a special mush produced in their throat called milk. After a week or two, the chick is a beautiful gray bird that can leave home and wander off to look for friends to play with. The parents let it do so because they have to look for food.

AND ALSO BECAUSE THE LITTLE ONES ARE SAFE, CONSTANTLY MONITORED BY THE ENTIRE COLONY.

THEY ARE up to 4.5 ft tall (1.4 m). **THEY WEIGH** up to 7.7 lbs (3.5 kg).

THEY LIVE near coasts in Asia, Central and South America, Africa, and the Mediterranean.

THEY EAT
mainly plankton, which gives them their typical pink color.

IN FACT, FLAMINGO COMMUNITIES ARE LIKE A LARGE FAMILY OF HUNDREDS AND HUNDREDS OF INDIVIDUALS WHO MAKE SURE THE CHICKS DON'T GET HURT.

THEIR NAME
means "with red feathers."

SEAHORSES

SCIENTIFIC NAME:
Hippocampus

Dad seahorse carries the eggs until the young are born.

A DAD WITH A BIG BELLY

When they decide to become parents, seahorses meet among waving strands of seaweed and marine plants. They get close to each other and touch, and for days they court each other with sinuous movements and by vibrating, lighting up with bright colors, and engaging in "dancing." When the right moment comes, the two rise toward the surface of the sea, moving in a spiral, almost like in a waltz. Then it happens in an instant, and it is something extremely rare in the world of fish. She lays her eggs in a sac inside his body, where they are fertilized. And so, swimming in shallow seas, you may happen to come across these "pregnant" males who wander around with their big bellies while giving oxygen, nourishment, and protection to the babies they carry. Theirs is exhausting work but necessary to raise their offspring.

THEY MUST EAT constantly, otherwise they could die.

THEY LIVE in seas all over the world, preferably among algae and marine plants.

AT THE TIME OF "BIRTH," THOUSANDS OF MINIATURE SEAHORSES CAN COME OUT OF THE FATHER, AND AFTER A QUICK GLANCE AT THEIR PARENTS, THEY IMMEDIATELY SWIM AWAY, PERFECTLY CAPABLE OF TAKING CARE OF THEMSELVES.

NOT ONLY SEAHORSES

The males of an African fish, the black-chinned tilapia, also carry the eggs, but they do so in their mouths.

LENGTH

0.39-13.7 inches (1-35 cm).

DESERT WOODLICE

SCIENTIFIC NAME: *Hemilepistus reaumuri*

Between parents and offspring, the union is also a matter of chemistry.

FAMILY SCENT

Woodlice, small terrestrial crustaceans that live in soil all over the globe, are not interested in their newborns. Except desert woodlice. The fathers and mothers of this species raise their many young and do so by forming inseparable pairs. You could say that they have no choice. In a desert, without care, the young would die instantly; being so united is essential for survival. The family of woodlice lives in a cool burrow up to a few feet deep, far from the terrible rays of the sun. And every day one of the two adults, in turn, goes in search of food. Returning home to their burrow with food might seem to be a problem because woodlice make identical burrows all very close to each other.

THE MOTHER keeps the eggs in a pouch so when they hatch she seems to be giving birth.

THEY LIVE in the deserts of North Africa and the Middle East.

BUT THE PARENTS DON'T GET CONFUSED BECAUSE THE HOLE OF EACH BURROW HAS A SPECIAL FRAGRANCE, THE SAME THAT EACH MEMBER OF THE FAMILY GIVES OFF.

IT IS A CHEMICAL SUBSTANCE THAT THEY ALL HAVE IN COMMON. IT IS THE SMELL OF HOME, THE SMELL OF FAMILY.

TERRIBLE NEIGHBORS

Among their main enemies are neighboring families!

TINY!

They are about 0.8 inches (20 mm) long.

CAPUCHIN MONKEYS

SCIENTIFIC NAME:
Sapajus libidinosus

Among certain animals, orphans are adopted even if they are of a different species.

A LUCKY ADOPTION

Among the bearded capuchin monkeys that live in the thickets of the Brazilian savannah, families are normally made up of a father and his many partners carrying their young. The babies either wrap themselves tightly around their mother's belly or they hold on to the hair on her back. In one case, however, a young capuchin monkey, while jumping from branch to branch, came across a baby marmoset, a small primate with expressive eyes and funny white tufts on the sides of its face. The marmoset had lost its family and would certainly die on its own. The capuchin carried the little monkey on her back. From that day on, the monkey learned to hold on to its new mother's fur and to grow up with her. If the other capuchin monkeys were initially disconcerted, it is certainly not common for animals of one species to adopt the little ones of another, they did not show it.

LUCKY
is a marmoset with white tufts.

AND THE YOUNG MARMOSET GREW UP HAPPILY IN ITS NEW ADOPTIVE FAMILY, SO MUCH SO THAT THE PEOPLE WHO FIRST OBSERVED HER GAVE HER A NAME: LUCKY.

FAMILIES
are made up of
12 to 20
individuals.

SIZE
Height: 16
inches (40 cm)
Weight: 4-6 lbs
(2-3 kg).

THERE ARE MANY TYPES OF FAMILIES!

As we have seen, different animals have different strategies for protecting their young. And the same species can have more than one strategy.

ALL FAMILIES ARE DIFFERENT

There are caresses given with tentacles and cuddles given with pecks; there are parents who only look after the eggs and others who spend a long time with their young; there are families with a single parent and others in which many adults participate in protecting the young.

BUT ALL FAMILIES ARE SIMILAR

Because they have only one goal at heart: to protect their young in the best, most suitable way for the environment in which they live.

THERE IS NO BETTER LESSON THAN WHAT CAN BE LEARNED FROM THE EXAMPLE OF ANIMALS. IT IS NOT SO MUCH THE TYPE OF FAMILY THAT MATTERS, BUT THE FACT THAT IT ACHIEVES THE MOST IMPORTANT GOAL: RAISING THE YOUNG SO THAT THEY CAN EVENTUALLY HEAD OUT ON THEIR OWN. AND THIS IS TRUE EVERYWHERE: IN THE SAVANNAHS AND FORESTS, IN THE DEPTHS OF THE SEA AND IN CITIES.

A FEW WORDS FROM SCIENCE

ETHOLOGY

Ethology is the science that studies the behavior of animals by comparing how one species behaves compared to another. The founder of this discipline is considered to be Austrian zoologist Konrad Lorenz (1903-1989) who in 1973 was awarded the Nobel Prize for his studies on geese.

STRATEGY R

This is the name for the type of animal that produces many offspring but then does not care for them, or at most only in the early stages, when the young are still in the eggs. A famous example is the mother turtle who lays her delicate eggs in the sand to protect them but then leaves the newly hatched turtles to fend for themselves against predators. The result is that many young are born, but a much smaller number survive.

STRATEGY K

This is the type of family that produces few offspring and then takes care of them by feeding them, defending them, and helping them until they grow up. Birds and mammals often behave this way. In these families, the mortality rate of the young is much lower than in "R" families.

POLYANDRY

Polyandry literally means "many males." It is when a female finds multiple mates. Generally, it is the males who take care of the offspring.

COOPERATIVE BREEDING

In many animal families, the care for the young is divided equally between the parents. In some, the breeding is done by a group made up of many mothers and fathers who organize themselves together. In others, however, there are individuals, called helpers, who do not have offspring but they help parents with theirs.

INDEPENDENT OFFSPRING

These are the young that are practically self-sufficient from birth or shortly after. This happens, for example, to many herbivorous mammals that, as soon as they are born, must be able to gallop with their parents and run away as fast as possible if a predator approaches.

DEPENDENT OFFSPRING

Often among predators, the little ones can afford to remain dependent on their parents for a long time. This can even last for many years, a time during which the body and brain develop best. Many monkeys have dependent infants because as soon as they are born, they cannot help but stay attached to their mothers while they jump from branch to branch. Among apes, but also among all animals, the human species is the one in which the young leave the family the latest.

POLYGYNY

Polygyny means "many females," and it is the opposite of polyandry. It occurs when a male mates with multiple females who have the task of taking care of the young.

ILLUSTRATOR

Francesco Faccia is an award-winning illustrator and comic artist. Franceso trained at the Academy of Fine Arts in Bologna, Italy, where he specialized in graphic design. Since then, Francesco has been working in the fields of visual arts and animation. He was the winner of the Lucca Junior 2022 illustration competition.

AUTHOR

Tecnoscienza is a group of authors and educators that has been involved in the dissemination of information on science, technology, mathematics, and the environment for numerous institutions, such as museums and companies, for more than 15 years. Their books, published in more than 20 countries, are designed to stimulate thoughts, actions, and emotions.

Graphic design and layout
Valentina Figus

Piazzale Luigi Cadorna, 6
20123 Milan, Italy
www.whitestar.it

Translation: Inga Sempel
Editing: Michele Suchomel-Casey

First printing, October 2025

ISBN 978-88-544-2159-2
1 2 3 4 5 6 29 28 27 26 25

Printed and manufactured by
Arkadas Printhouse
Ankara Turkey

FSC www.fsc.org MIX Paper | Supporting responsible forestry FSC® C178000